GLENDA AUSTIN

ABOUT THE SERIES

The Composer's Choice series showcases piano works by an exclusive group of composers. Each collection contains classic piano pieces that were carefully chosen by the composer, as well as brand-new pieces written especially for the series. Helpful performance notes are also included.

ISBN 978-1-4803-9529-9

WILLIS MUSIC

Exclusively Distributed By

HAL•LEONARD®
CORPORATION

7777 W. BLUEMOUND RD. P.O. BOX 13819 MILWAUKEE, WI 53213

Visit Hal Leonard Online at
www.halleonard.com

FROM THE COMPOSER

For this elementary volume of my Composer's Choice, I've chosen some pieces that were first published more than 15 years ago! Yes, I know that in the bigger scheme of print music, that's not a terribly long time, but to me, it seems OLD! It was fun re-visiting them and getting to know them again. But, in addition to the oldies, I've written two brand-new solos: "The Plucky Penguin" and "Betcha-Can Boogie." I can only hope they will last for 15 years, if not longer. Please enjoy every solo in this book; I've had a great time playing them all this evening!

Glenda Austin

May 19, 2014

CONTENTS

BY GLENDA AUSTIN

BETCHA-CAN BOOGIE

"Betcha-Can Boogie" proves that anyone can boogie! Keep it light and detached. Start by learning it slowly, and then increase to a comfortable tempo: the faster, the better!

THE PLUCKY PENGUIN

Penguins are a group of flightless, aquatic birds, and many of them live in Antarctica. They are highly adapted for life in the water, their wings more like flippers. My plucky penguin is spunky, cheerful and spirited. Though a bit awkward, his walk is confident, steady, and he always arrives on time. Play this piece with the same characteristics: spunky, cheerful and spirited.

SHADOW TAG

"Shadow Tag" is a variation of the classic childhood game, tag. The tricky part about it is that you can't feel if you've been tagged: it's your SHADOW that has to be tagged. This short piece is played quickly and lightly. The interval jumps at the end of most measures represent the "tagging" of the shadow.

ROLLING CLOUDS

Cumulus clouds are big puffy clouds that look like floating pieces of cotton. In "Rolling Clouds," think of giant cumulus clouds everywhere, gently moving toward each other to make even bigger cumulus clouds. In this short piece, rain threatens but never comes; and in measures 21-24, the sun peeks through—only to hide back behind the big rolling clouds. Play it legato, evenly and dramatically.

JIVIN' AROUND

The word *jive* is associated with swing music and early jazz, which is lively, fun and popular with everyone. "Jivin' Around" is exactly that—have fun with it!

SUNSET OVER THE SEA

This piece suggests calm water with a few gently rolling waves. Imagine it is dusk: the sunset is beautiful and the sea is tranquil. Play smoothly, in a relaxed and gentle manner.

SOUTHPAW SWING

Southpaw is a slang word for a left-handed person. I happen to be left-handed, and this piece features the left hand in a jazzy motif. Bring it out and play with precision, though it need not be too fast. I hope right-handers will find this piece to be a great exercise, but we southpaws will definitely excel!

TARANTELLA (SPIDER AT MIDNIGHT)

A lively dance from Italy is a *tarantella*. Please play my tarantella lightly and quickly! In the Coda, accelerate the tempo as much as possible. In my mind, this particular spider-at-midnight is just a harmless little arachnid trying to spin a web in order to catch some dinner.

Betcha-Can Boogie

Glenda Austin

Play detached

2nd time to Coda

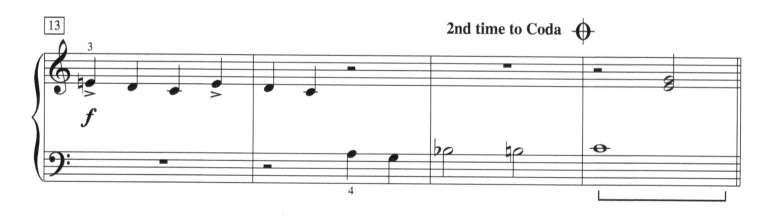

The Plucky Penguin

Glenda Austin

© 2014 by The Willis Music Co.
International Copyright Secured   All Rights Reserved

2nd time to Coda ⊕

D.C. al Coda

CODA
⊕

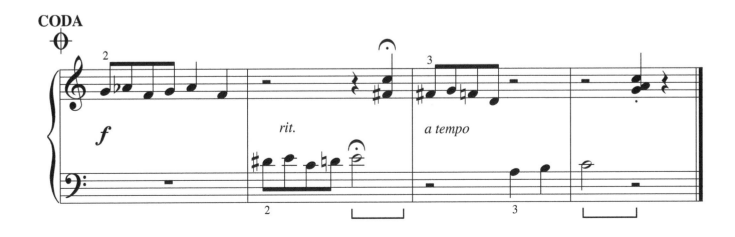

Shadow Tag

Glenda Austin

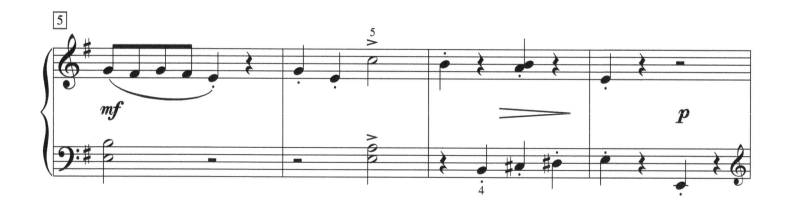

Rolling Clouds

Glenda Austin

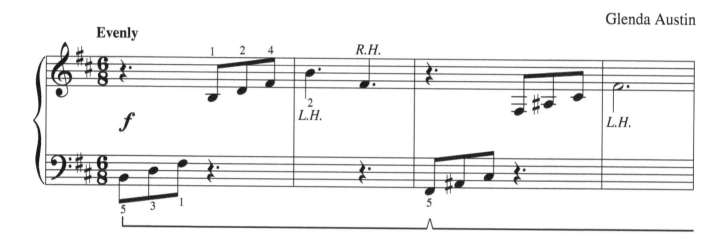

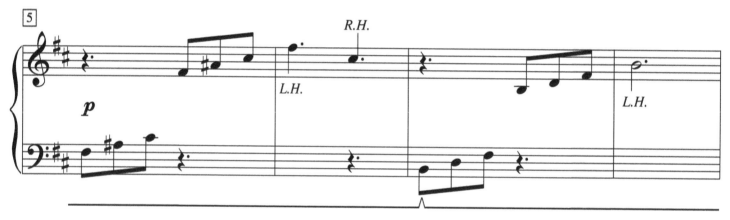

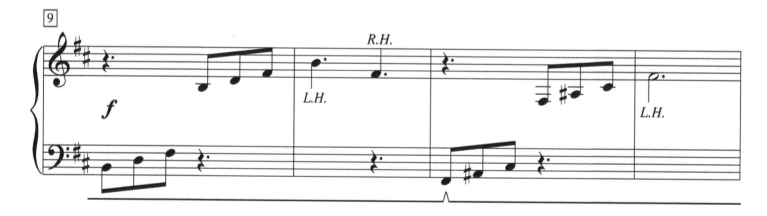

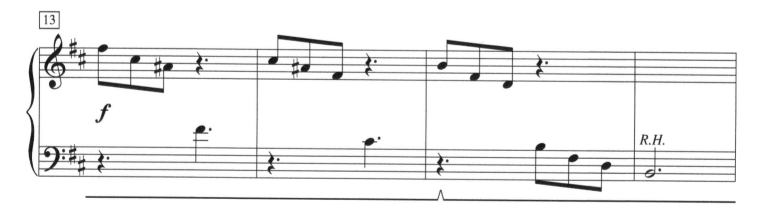

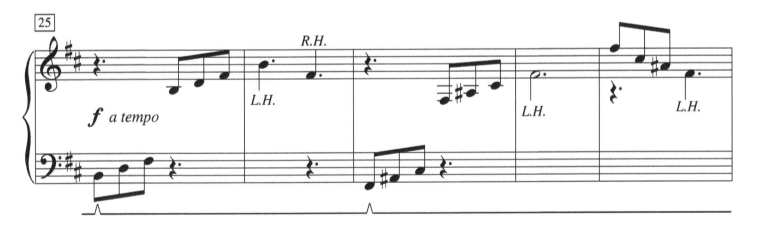

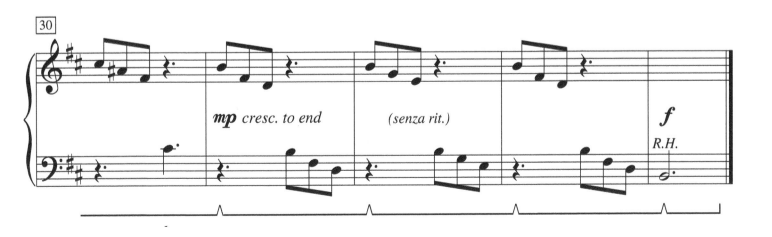

Jivin' Around

for Susan Horton

Glenda Austin

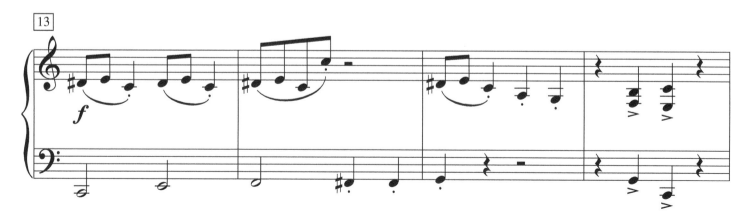

Sunset Over the Sea

Glenda Austin

Southpaw Swing

Glenda Austin

With precision

2nd time to Coda ⊕

Tarantella
(Spider at Midnight)

for Kevin Costley

Glenda Austin

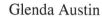

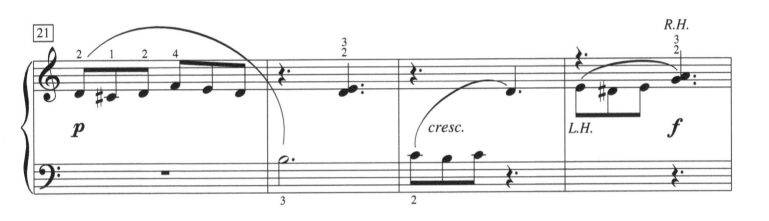

D.C. al Coda

CODA

As fast as you can to the end!

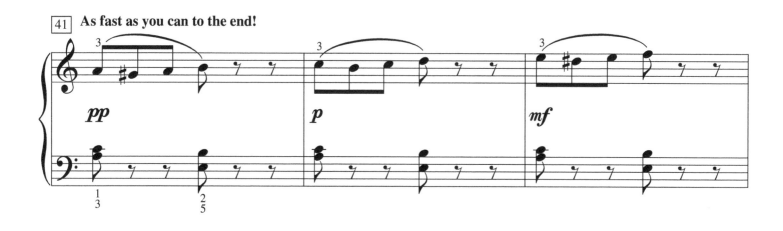